Love at Home
Starring
GRANDPA

Love at Home
Starring
GRANDPA

George D. Durrant

Bookcraft
Salt Lake City, Utah

Library of Congress Catalog Card Number: 95-81232
ISBN 1-57008-197-2

First Printing, 1995

Printed in the United States of America

Contents

Chapter One

A Very Important Person

"Grandpa. Grandpa! *Grandpa!* Are you awake?"

If I hadn't been, I was now. It was five-thirty in the morning in Houston, Texas. Just two days after Christmas.

As I forced open my eyes, I saw my four-year-old grandson, Kolby, standing at my side and studiously staring at me to see if there were any signs of life. Seeing his face through the dimness of the early morning light was like seeing the sun come up, and suddenly I could answer with great enthusiasm, "Yes sirree, Kolby! Your grandpa is wide awake."

"Get up, Grandpa. It's time to play."

Five minutes later I was sitting on the front room floor pushing Thomas the Tank Engine down his wooden track as Kolby, who sat at my side, drew Thomas on his Etch A Sketch. It was for moments like this that I had made the long journey from my home in Provo, Utah, to Kolby's house in Houston, Texas. It was for moments like this that I thanked the Lord for the joy and privilege of being Grandpa.

As I looked at what my grandson was drawing on the Etch A Sketch, I was intrigued by how that little machine worked, and I said to Kolby, "I get to play with the Etch A Sketch next. Okay?"

"Okay, Grandpa. I'll be through in a minute. Then I'll let you have a turn. Right now you just keep pushing Thomas, okay?"

"Okay," I said with a little feeling of impatience.

As I looked at Kolby's excited expression my heart welled up with love for him, and I reached out and pulled him close to me and said, "Grandpa needs a hug from his friend named Kolby."

"Don't hug me right now, Grandpa. You made me make a line that I didn't want to make."

As he pulled away I asked him, "How come I love you so much, Kolby?"

He laughed and said, "I don't know." He then quickly added, "Maybe it is because I let you play with my toys." I smiled and thought to myself, *That is only a part of the reason. There is more to it than that. Much more.* But this serious thought was not for now, so I turned and pushed Thomas the Tank Engine down the track past Sir Topham Hatt, the railroad superintendent.

I found myself being glad that Kolby's parents were

still sound asleep. We had all been up late the night before, and so they needed their rest. But the greatest reason I was glad was that I could have Kolby all to myself. And that was a bit like being in heaven without dying. The only thing that marred those golden moments was my longing to get hold of the Etch A Sketch. And maybe soon even that would happen.

I had come to Houston two days earlier, on Christmas night. Marilyn had not come with me, because we had decided that she should stay at home during the holidays so that the other grandchildren could come to our house.

My trip to Houston had been planned for two months. We had learned that our daughter Sarah and her husband, Kelly, could not come to Utah for Christmas. The only way we could soothe the pain of their not being with us was for me to go there.

When I called to tell Sarah that I would be coming, she announced it to Kolby. Each morning from that time on, when he would wake up, he would ask his mother, "Is Grandpa George coming today?" Each day he would be disappointed as his mother would try to explain to him that I would not come until Christmas Day. I felt sorry for him because we all know how hard it is to wait for Christmas, especially if you are only four years old.

But time, as it does, had gone by, and soon it was just a week until Christmas. Kolby could sense that Christmas was nigh at hand and that Grandpa would soon be there.

Sarah phoned me six days before Christmas and told me that Kolby didn't care whether or not Santa Claus came—all he cared about was that Grandpa was coming. After she and I talked, she let Kolby talk to me. He was so excited that I could scarcely understand his words. But I did pick up enough of his message to know that he had plans for him and me to go buy a truck at Fred Meyer, to play in the sandpile in the park, to watch some Thomas the Tank Engine videos, and to go to the children's museum.

The next few days of waiting were long for both Kolby and me. During those days, I tried to go to bed early and to eat a nutritious diet. I didn't want to get sick so that I couldn't go. I couldn't let Kolby down. When I'd drive, I'd do so with extreme care so that I wouldn't get hurt in an accident. If, while walking, I crossed a road, I'd look both ways several times for oncoming traffic so that I wouldn't get hit by a car. I had too much to live for to take any chances.

Finally Christmas came. Most of our children live near us, so it was with great joy that I got to see most of them on Christmas morning. We had a lovely Christmas dinner at my son Warren's house. Finally it was time for me to go to the airport in Salt Lake City.

During the long flight to Houston, I tried to read from a book I had, but I was too keyed up to concentrate. Sleep was out of the question.

As the plane touched down, I had to deliberately take several deep breaths to calm myself down. This was no time to have a heart attack. Not when I was this close to Kolby.

I got off the airplane ahead of most of the other people

who were on board. I usually try to be a gentleman and let others go before me. But this time no one on board had so great a reason as I did to want to push ahead. Finally I was in that tunnel-like thing that leads from the plane to the terminal.

Then I saw Sarah. And there at her side was Kolby. When he saw me he rushed forward. I knelt down so that he and I would be the same height. He shouted, "Grandpa! Grandpa!"

And I shouted back, "Kolby, my grandson!" I took him in my arms and I was happy.

So that is the story of my arrival in Houston. That is the joyous part of the story. But there is a sad part also. After being with this wonderful family for a week, it was nearly time to say good-bye. The next day I would be going home.

That last day was a bittersweet day. It was sweet because Kolby and I had become even dearer friends, and that increased our joy as we pushed Thomas the Tank Engine and as we walked to the sandpile in the park. But inside each golden moment was the dark thought that tomorrow I would have to leave him.

Kolby did not know that I was going. I pleaded with his parents not to tell him. But that night as we ate supper, his mother gently announced, "Kolby, tomorrow Grandpa has to go home." I watched his face and was a little disappointed to not notice any great concern in his expression. I didn't eat much because of my sadness, and I noticed that Kolby didn't either.

After we had eaten, Kolby did not want to play. His

disposition had changed. His fun-loving nature had gone out of him. I sensed, as did his mother, that the news of my leaving had hurt him deep within his heart.

That night, when he was asleep, we planned my early morning journey to the airport. I asked that Kolby not come as it would be too difficult for me to say good-bye to him there.

But the next morning he was awake and there was no way to keep him from going. He loved the airport.

Finally, as the last boarding call was made, I gave each of the family an embrace as I told them of my love. I then bade them each good-bye. Last of all, I held Kolby close to me and said, "Good-bye, my dear little friend. I love you with all my heart."

He didn't cry, nor did I. I walked away, and just as I was going to go out of his sight, I looked back. My eyes met his. Something went between us that can only go between those who each have some of the other within him. The longing to have me stay with him that I saw in his eyes cut a quick path from my eyes to my heart, and I began to cry.

There is a children's song that says, "I am a very important person." That trip to Texas proved to me that I am a very important person. Maybe I'm not so very important to some people, but I sure am important to my family, and especially to my grandchildren. And there is nothing so joyous to me as making them happy when I come and sad when I leave.

So now I say to each of you other grandpas, "You are a very important person." That is what this book is all about. Don't sleep through the opportunities that could be yours in being a grandfather by playing golf too much or going south for the winter when your grandchildren are in the north. Put your family first. Go see the grandkids every chance you get. If you do, you'll really be a very important person. If you put other things in your life before them, you will just be a sort of important person but not really a very important person.

Now is the time, while you are able, and before that last good-bye at the eternal airport, to truly be a grandpa. How would you answer the question "Grandpa. Grandpa! *Grandpa!* Are you awake?"

Chapter Two

A Grandpa for
Every Child

I was at a business luncheon with three work associates at a lovely canyon restaurant. Three ladies sat at a nearby table. It was obvious that they were dear friends or perhaps sisters because they were eagerly and enthusiastically conversing with each other. One of the three had a beautiful baby boy who appeared to be about nine months old. The baby, who was seated in a high chair, had been happily enjoying himself. But now he began to be a bit fussy. The mother gave him a plastic rattle, which quieted him enough that she could turn back to the conversation. But after a short time he threw the rattle down and began to cry. She tried to calm him but he would not be calmed. I could see the frustration on her face as she longed for him to be contented so that she could continue the good time that she was obviously having with her friends. But the baby persisted in demanding her attention.

At that moment, I lost all interest in what was going on at my table. I had a great longing as I looked at that little guy. I found myself wishing with all my heart that I was his grandpa. If I had been, I could have walked to where he was, lifted him up from his chair, told his mom to have a good time, and taken him out to see the ducks on the nearby pond. If I could have done that, it would have made three people very happy: the baby's mom, the baby, and me—his grandpa. But none of that could happen because I was not the little boy's grandpa. And that, for just that brief moment, made a little crack in my heart.

That experience made me think to myself, *Oh, how I wish that I could be every little child's grandpa.* I wouldn't want to be every child's father. That would be too much work and too much responsibility. No man could handle such an enormous task. But it would be possible to be every child's grandpa. All that would take would be love, and there is always enough of that to reach every child—no matter how many.

But because I can't have that wish of being every child's grandpa, my other wish is that every little child could have a grandpa. One who loved him enough to go to where he is, sweep him up into his arms, and take him to see the ducks. Sometimes I think the reason there are ponds and ducks is so that grandpas can take their grandchildren to see them and can say, "See the ducks."

Of course, if that little imagined grandson I took out of the restaurant to the pond got tired of being with me and started to cry, I'd hurry him right back to his mother and go on my way to do other things. That is the way it is with grandpas; they can have all the fun of the good times without all the work or responsibility of the other times.

I have heard it said that every child needs to spend some time each day or so with someone who is crazy about her. That someone is grandpa. Just go to a grandchild's house or have him come to your house. Then for a moment or two—or longer—sit with the child, go for a walk with him, pet the dog with her, pull him in a wagon, push her in a swing, draw pictures and color with him, look up at an airplane or a bird or a cloud with her, read a story to him.

In any one of a million ways, show and tell each grandchild that you love him or her with a perfect love. In these brief moments you don't need to run with him, swing her around, hike steep hills, or play vigorous games. That is for young parents who still have energy to burn. A grandparent's most valuable time and effort should be the quiet times where love is more important than excitement. In your moments with your grandchildren you don't need to discipline them. That is parents' work. Not grandpa's work.

Grandpa's work is to look beyond any faults that his grandchildren might have and to see only their wonderful nature and the divine potential that is really in them. Grandpa's role is to tell them how beautiful they are, how good they are at throwing a ball, how well they read, how much you like their piano solo, how well they color with their Crayolas, how good the snake is that they made out of Play-Doh, how much they help their mom and dad, how much you love them.

I'm making this sound like all grandchildren are very young. But these same principles are true if they are in their teens. Grandpa's affirming words and actions when the grandchildren are teenagers might make the very difference in the direction that they choose to take their lives. Many times, when they are upset at their parents, Grandpa, without being judgmental or interfering with parental discipline, can love them into taking the good path.

Every child wears a sign that says, "I want to be important now." It is when no one reads that sign that the child begins to lose part of his or her wonderful inward self. Grandpa's privilege is to read and respond to that sign every time he sees the child and to make the child feel that he or she is the most important person in the world.

If there are two or more children in the family, Grandpa can figure out and do something that shows love to each child. Often, just one minute is all it takes. It is not enough to say, "I love all four of you kids." Somehow you have to get to each one, and in a very private way, say, "You are really getting to be a great reader. How did you learn to read so well? I'll bet that you are your teacher's favorite. You sure are a favorite of mine."

Or, go to a grandson doing his homework in his room and say, "Hey, I can tell by the way that you study that someday you'll be another Einstein. I'd better not disturb such a scholar, but I couldn't leave without telling you how proud I am to be your grandpa."

Or, take a child who is just learning to talk into your arms and go outside to find a bird. I think it should be illegal for anyone except Grandpa to show a little grandchild his first bird—to point at the bird and say, "Bird. Pretty bird. Can you say *bird?* Oh, good, you said *bird.* Grandpa and you love the bird, the pretty bird."

Or, hold a little child and say, "I wish that I could take you home. We'd play. Then we would eat ice cream and then we would go to the park, and then we'd eat hot dogs and potato chips and olives. We'd have so much fun! Grandpa loves you, but you'd better stay here, or your mommy and daddy would cry and cry and cry because they would miss you so much. For they love you just like I do."

Oh, how I wish every child could have a grandpa who would do the things that I have just described! I wish I could do as well as I have made it sound. But sometimes I'm too tired or I have too much else to do, and I don't do as well as a grandpa ought to do. But from now on I'll try to do better. How about you?

Chapter Three

The Grandfather Spirit

I never knew one of my two grandfathers. He died long before I was born. I don't remember with my mind the other one, who died when I was one year old. But somehow I remember him with my heart. I'm told that he would come to our house and take me for a ride in my baby buggy. I'm sure he thought that I was a very cute little fellow, because he did have good eyesight. I'm sure that he said to me, "Bird. Pretty bird. Georgie, can you say *bird?* Oh, good, you said *bird*. Grandpa and you love the bird, the pretty bird."

But though I do not remember my grandfathers with my mind, all through my life I have felt their spirits. And my heart has turned to them with a great longing to someday be with them. To be loved by them, as I love my grandchildren—their great-great-grandchildren. And when my grandchildren and I are finally with them, we will all sit and watch the birds and talk of dear things—family things.

I recall a few years ago I tried to write the history of my Grandfather Durrant. Just about all those who had ever known him were dead, and so I couldn't ask anybody about him. I searched all the records that I could find, but they were all factual and merely told about what he had done. They didn't tell me much of who he really was.

I did learn that he was troubled by a drinking problem. He drifted from job to job. I learned that he had been a kindly father who longed for his children to do better than he felt he had done.

The most complete description of his life that I could find was recorded in his obituary. There the writer summarized Grandpa's life by saying, "This man was neither prominent in the Church nor in the community." When I read those words I cast the paper aside and said in a loud and objecting voice, "Well, he was prominent to me!"

I believe my grandpa was grateful for my attitude toward him, because one time in a very quiet and private moment of my life, he gently came to me. To my heart he said, "George, I don't know if you are proud of me. But I'm sure proud of you."

Isn't that just like a grandpa to say such a thing? That is the spirit of a grandpa. And when he said that, I wanted to shout loud enough for all heaven to hear, "Grandpa, I'm so proud of you that I can scarcely contain my joy."

It would not have been a much more difficult thing for

my grandpa to come from the other side of the veil to visit me than it was for me to visit my grandchildren on one special occasion. The circumstances of that visit were these:

I accepted an opportunity to speak in Missouri on Friday and Saturday night because the places where I was to speak were not too far from where my daughter Marinda, her husband, Steve, and their three little children lived in southern Indiana.

After my Saturday evening address, which concluded at nine o'clock, I jumped in my rental car and headed from Missouri to Indiana to visit this family, whom I had not seen in nearly nine months. I drove until midnight and sang all the way. I couldn't help singing for joy, because every minute of the journey I could see little five-year-old Lexie, three-year-old Ben, and little six-month-old Tyler in my mind and in my heart. With such a vision in my mind I did not want to stop, but wisdom dictated that I stop at a motel and get a few hours of sleep.

At four in the morning, I was on the road again. I passed by the big arch at St. Louis and crossed the bridge that spanned the Mississippi. Now I was on a highway that led directly to Jeffersonville, Indiana, where my wonderful family anxiously awaited the arrival of Grandpa.

As I whizzed along I took great pleasure in seeing the signs which indicated how far it was to Jeffersonville. One hundred miles, then sixty-five, then forty, then twenty. By now I could not restrain my joy. I sang and whistled and talked out loud. Soon I was less than one-half hour away from pure happiness. Finally I was at the exit, then on the river road, then at the turnoff. Then I could see the house. A few minutes later I was greeted at the door by that wonderful salutation, "Grandpa. Grandpa! *Grandpa!*" I was with people that I love more than life itself. I cannot begin to say how much joy my presence brought to that little family who were so starved for family and for home and for Grandpa.

I could only stay the afternoon and the evening. At four in the morning I'd head up the road that I had come down—back to St. Louis to catch a flight home and to get back to my teaching post.

When it was bedtime I went to the children's room to tell them stories. But before the stories Lexie and Ben began to jump up and down on Lexie's bed. Their mother scolded them and told them to stop. So I decided to take everything into my own hands and to make everything all right. Soon I was standing on the bed beside the two little ones, and seconds later I was jumping up and down with them. Neither they nor I could stop laughing, even though my daughter tried to act exasperated. Then, she too gave up and joined in the fun.

The next morning, I quietly arose so as to not wake any of them. I went to the children's room. They were fast asleep. I kissed Ben on the cheek and then little Tyler and finally Princess Lexie. It was as if I were kissing angels. I turned away and was soon out the door and in my car. I could not hold back the tears that are so much a part of saying sweet good-byes.

Some, upon hearing of my long journey, questioned why I'd driven such a long distance for just eight waking hours with this little group of people. They didn't know nor understand that at that time these were the ones in our family who needed Grandpa the most. And because of that, these were the ones Grandpa needed the most. That, then, is the spirit that goes with being or having a grandpa. Somehow, Grandpa will come to see those who need him most–those who are most lonely, those who most need encouragement. Sometimes we may not even know that he has come. But somehow, because he came and quietly kissed us on the cheek, he brought to us the spirit of Grandpa. And because of that, things always get better.

Chapter Four

Grandfather Abraham

On May 29, 1980, I wrote in my journal:

> This is a red-letter day. This afternoon I became a grand-
> father. Matt and Jackie had a little baby son. Mother and
> child are fine, and Grandfather has a wonderful feeling. I
> haven't seen the little fellow yet, but already he has a spe-
> cial place in my heart. He will be called Jacob.

There was once another Jacob. His grandfather was
named Abraham—the great and noble man who was the
father of the covenant people. So, on that special day
when my Jacob was born, I, in a sense, became like unto
Abraham.

Jesus Christ is our model for individual life, and the

family of Abraham, Isaac, and Jacob is our model for family life. When I think of this wonderful patriarchal family, I see each of them in various stages of their lives. I picture young Jacob—the grandson—as the model for a young adult. Isaac—the mature son—is my model for fatherhood. And Abraham—the venerable patriarch—is my model for a grandfather.

As I think back upon the stages of my adult life, I first see myself as a young Jacob. Then, as those years so swiftly passed beneath my feet, I evolved into the maturity of father Isaac; and finally, and almost suddenly, I now see myself as grandfather Abraham.

As a young man I had once been like unto Jacob. You remember the problems that he had with his brother Esau over the birthright. Because of these bad feelings and because his parents desired him to marry within his faith, he left the comforts of home and went on a most important mission. Of this experience the Bible says:

> And Jacob went out from Beer-sheba, and went toward Haran.
>
> And he lighted upon a certain place, and tarried there all night, because the sun was set; and he took of the stones of that place, and put them for his pillows, and lay down in that place to sleep.
>
> And he dreamed, and behold a ladder set up on the earth, and the top of it reached to heaven: and behold the angels of God ascending and descending on it.
>
> And, behold, the Lord stood above it, and said, I am the Lord God of Abraham thy father, and the God of Isaac: the land whereon thou liest, to thee will I give it, and to thy seed. (Genesis 28:10–13.)

I too as a young man had gone away from my home to do the will of God. In the early days of my mission to England, I, like Jacob, came to a land which was at first a strange land to me. I, like Jacob, had been lonely for family and for home. I, like Jacob, in a sense found in that holy place the vision of the ladder that leads to heaven. I, like Jacob, was never the same person after that vision, which came to me slowly but surely through a multitude of sacred experiences in England, the land of my fathers. My gentle vision of the way to reach heaven, like Jacob's more dramatic vision of the ladder, showed me the way to extend my upward reach toward heaven.

At the end of my mission in England, I, in my own way, vowed a vow as did Jacob. A vow about how I would live my life.

And Jacob vowed a vow, saying, If God will be with me, and will keep me in this way that I go, and will give me bread to eat, and raiment to put on,

So that I come again to my father's house in peace; then shall the Lord be my God:

And this stone, which I have set for a pillar, shall be God's house: and of all that thou shalt give me I will surely give the tenth unto thee (Genesis 28:20–22).

I desired with all my heart for the Lord to be my God. And I too vowed to give a tenth unto him.

A few years later, I became an Isaac—a young father. You recall the beautiful story of how Rebekah was found for Isaac in a distant land. That happened because Abraham longed to preserve the covenant heritage by having his son marry a woman of the true faith. Because this was not possible in the land where the family lived, Abraham sent his trusted servant to the land of his relatives to find a bride for Isaac.

The servant soon set out on that historic journey. Then, having arrived at the far-off land to which he had been sent, the servant sought the Lord's affirmation as to whom he was to choose. The servant asked that the woman who would give him and also his camels water to drink be the chosen one.

Rebekah came to the well where the servant waited. He asked for a drink, which she graciously gave him. Of this event the Bible tells us:

> And the damsel was very fair to look upon . . . and she went down to the well, and filled her pitcher, and came up. . . .
> And when she had done giving him drink, she said, I will draw water for thy camels also, until they have done drinking. (Genesis 24:16, 19.)

From this brief account, we all fall in love with this magnificent woman.

I too married a girl whom the Lord had chosen for me from a distant land. For, you see, I lived in American Fork, and Marilyn lived in the strange and distant land called Salt Lake City.

Married to a woman with the qualities and virtues of Rebekah, I, as did Isaac, became a father. I wanted to be a gentle, loving father, as was Isaac. A father who modeled all that was good for his children. A man of peace, who loved and was loved by all who knew him.

The years passed quickly. And then, with the birth of my little Jacob, it was time for me to become an Abraham—a grandfather, a patriarch.

My grandson Jacob is fifteen years old as I write this book. Jacob, the son of Isaac, was about fifteen years old when Abraham died. The Bible does not say that Jacob was fifteen, but I figured it out. You see, Abraham was one hundred years old when Isaac was born. Isaac was sixty years old when Jacob was born. Abraham died at age one hundred seventy-five. So, Jacob was about fifteen when Abraham died.

I bring this up because I'm glad my model for being a grandfather, Abraham, had the joy of his little grandson Jacob for fifteen wonderful years, just as I have had with my grandson Jacob. I know that his Jacob was as dear to him as my grandson Jacob is to me. The emotions of being a grandfather are the same in all generations of time and will be throughout all eternity.

Generally our time on earth spans three generations—grandparents, parents, and children. Of course there are exceptions. For sometimes children grow up without grandparents. And on the other hand, there is often a fourth generation in a family. Those in this generation are called great-grandparents. To me, it is sad when children do not have the blessing of living grandparents. Children don't miss grandparents whom they never knew, because that is not the way things are. But when they do have grandparents it is such an added blessing to family life. And when they have great-grandparents it is a most sacred blessing. Sometimes I think that it is a great mistake for parents to move to places where they and the children are at a great distance from the grandparents.

The opportunities for employment should not outweigh the blessings of intergenerational love and togetherness.

When I think of the three-generation family, I think of myself, the grandfather; Devin, the father; and little Ryan, the grandson. I could think of other such models in my family; but something special happened with Ryan, Devin, and me. You see, I was born on October 20, 1931. Devin was born on October 20, 1960. And Ryan was born on October 20, 1991. Can you imagine the thrill that came to me when my son was born on my birthday? Then came the added joy when, almost unbelievably, on my birthday, and on my son Devin's birthday, I received word that Devin's wife, Julie, was in the hospital in Orem and had just given birth to a little son. Not even my hero Abraham could equal such a three-generation phenomenon.

There is something indefinably wonderful about the three-generation family. Whenever such families gather or write or phone or speak of each other, we hear the glorious titles: son, daughter, brother, sister, mother, father, uncle, aunt, cousin, and the most honored of all the titles—grandfather and grandmother, grandma and grandpa. All of these titles, and the people who bear them, when added together equal the most heart-touching of all titles—the title *family.*

The interrelationship of all these people is centered in the dearest of all the heart's places—the place that we call *home.* Home and family, coupled together, are the essence of happiness, the hope of the world, and the binding hope of the eternal future.

It is good to be a son—a Jacob. It is good to be a daughter—a Rachel. It is good to be a father—an Isaac. It is good to be a mother—a Rebekah. But the Lord saves the best until last, for the crown of life's joys comes when we become as Sarah and as Abraham, when we become Grandma and Grandpa.

But with great blessings come great responsibilities. It is not enough just to be called Grandpa. We must in very deed be Grandpa.

Mothers and fathers have the responsibility to raise the children to adulthood, but Grandma and Grandpa have the privilege of helping the parents to raise the grandchildren to great heights—to not only see the grandchildren as they are but see them as they can be and, through family love, will be.

It is the responsibility of you as Grandpa to stand on holy ground, and to prayerfully and diligently lift the grandchildren to that ground. You, as a grandpa, do not have to be perfect, but you need to want to be. And if that is your desire, the Lord will lift you up, and in the eyes of your grandchildren you will be perfect.

Abraham and Sarah, Isaac and Rebekah, and Jacob and Rachel, we honor your very names. We know you had heart-breaking family problems while you lived on earth, just as we sometimes do. We know that you are in your exalted places in heaven. We know that we have the potential to join you there. It is our hope that our hearts will forever turn to you as our models and to you as our parents. For we know that we are of Israel. We know that we are your family. We long to leave to our descendants the faith and the integrity and the love which you left to us.

I sometimes call my grandson Jacob by the name

Israel. For that was the name Abraham's grandson was called by the Lord. And it is my hope for my grandson Jacob and for all of my grandchildren that each of them will, with the blessing promised to Israel, be a prince or a princess in the Lord's earthly kingdom and that each will have power with God and with their fellowmen. May you and I, as grandpas, help our grandchildren, our young Israelites, to have such power and such rich blessings.

Chapter Five

Relying
on Grandmother

One year a terrible thought crept into the minds of our family. Someone proposed that we all go out to a restaurant to eat Thanksgiving dinner. Grandmother Marilyn even jumped on the bandwagon. They had the momentum of a team of runaway horses. It took all the power and ingenuity that I could muster to first slow the idea down and then to finally stop it and turn it around.

Thanksgiving dinner away from home! I couldn't bear the thought. That would mean that the grandchildren and the children couldn't head over the river and through the woods to Grandma's house. It would mean that we wouldn't have Grandma's hot rolls. I've never had one of those rolls melt in my mouth without believing that I was in heaven. It would mean that the turkey dressing would be made by someone who didn't fully understand the sacred nature and the perfect blending of the fine ingredients of that perfect food. It would mean that the gravy would be stirred by hands other than Grandma's masterful hands.

But more than that it would mean that the grandkids couldn't come and see their cousins and the turkey and the three tables that fill two rooms. They couldn't enjoy the combined emotional frenzy caused by the double excitement of both seeing their cousins and looking forward to the delicious meal that would soon follow—the very smell of which could give the family a desire which could send all of them out of their minds. And besides, Thanksgiving food just doesn't taste right if it isn't flavored by the atmosphere of Grandma's house.

If we went out to eat, after dinner we couldn't all push back our chairs and just sit around in a daze and half sleep and half talk. Sure the family could eat at a restaurant and then come over to Grandma's house. But that is like going to a gymnasium when the basketball game is already over.

There is no place at a restaurant where I could sit on a couch and hold the newest little grandchild on my lap and for a moment or two hug him or her in complete security. In a public place, I couldn't find a quiet corner and a special moment to tell each granddaughter and each grandson of my love for him or her and let them know of their unique place in my heart.

But of course this is all easy for me to say. On Thanksgiving Day, I help out by setting up the tables and chairs. But it is Grandma who gets out of bed before dawn to put the turkey in the oven. It is Grandma who does the masterful work involved in creating the dressing and the rolls. Sure the kids bring some items, but the real responsibility is on Grandma.

It would be impossible for me to be Grandpa at Thanksgiving if it weren't for the selfless service of Grandma. I couldn't be Grandpa on any day if it weren't for the caring of Grandma. It is no wonder that everyone loves her in a slightly different and in a little deeper way than they love me. I always rely on Grandma to be the main event. I'm just a wonderful sideshow.

I don't know how long Grandma can keep making my Thanksgiving dreams come true. All I can do is hope that it will go on for another twenty years. I know that the decision to go to one of our children's houses or to a restaurant for Thanksgiving dinner will come someday. But, even then, I'll keep making my appeal to stay at home. It is so much easier to be Grandpa when everybody is in Grandma's house, and the food is on the table, and the whole house is filled with family love.

But my real point in talking about Thanksgiving is not to talk about food and fun. My point is that almost all that I long to do as Grandpa is reliant on the things that Grandma does as Grandma.

I recall that once she was in England with our daughter Kathryn on a vacation to celebrate Kathryn's graduation from high school. At home, some of the children and grandchildren and I went on a picnic. We had a good time, but I felt like I was only half there. I'd just automatically look for Marilyn, and then I'd realize that she wasn't there and I'd lose my power to really be Grandpa.

Sometimes when Marilyn and I are at home together, certain of our grandchildren come into my mind and heart. I get up, go to the phone, and call them. I say something such as, "Hello, this is Grandpa George."

Then I talk to little four-year-old Eliza by asking, "What are you doing?" She answers. I tell her that I love her. Then I say, "I wish I was at your house so that we could play and eat ice cream." And then I'm really out of ideas. So I ask to talk to little Annie. I ask Annie the same things, and then I ask to talk to their mom or their dad. After thirty seconds of talking to Mom or Dad, I can't think of anything else to say. I'm just not good at talking on the phone. But then I get to the real purpose of my call. I say to the parent that I'm talking to, "Grandma wants to talk to you." I give her the phone and she talks to them and talks to them and talks to them. On and on it goes. She really is a master at talking on the phone.

The longer the conversation goes, the more I like it. Because I feel that if they can talk to Grandma Marilyn, then all will be well with this little family who mean so much to me. When she finally hangs up, I go to her and ask, "What did they say?"

She replies, "Why are you asking me? You talked to them."

I reply, "But I didn't know what to say. You know I can't talk on the phone. Tell me what they said to you."

Then she gives me a report on all that they said. As she does so, I thrill at her every word.

It seems as if everything is like that. I'm good at the mountain peaks of grandparenting, but she covers the matters which have great depth. The best thing that I do as Grandpa is to help the grandkids and their parents to come in frequent contact with Grandma.

Thus, before I go on with this book I want to give credit where credit is really due—to Grandma.

My dream is that I will be able to forever feel the spirit of Thanksgiving at home with the family. And I know that I will have those dear feelings on Thanksgiving Day, and every other day, whenever Grandmother Marilyn is there to make it all happen.

Chapter Six

Grandpa's Best Gift

I recall the days when I was a young father and my children were under the age of ten. I was smarter than they were in those days. I used to trick them. My grandchildren love it when I tell the stories of how I used to trick their dad or their mom.

One story the grandchildren like is the story of the watermelon. You see, I had planted some watermelon plants in the garden. I didn't garden so well, and so when fall came and it was nearly harvesttime there wasn't a sign of a watermelon on any of my vines. The children were really disappointed by that. So one night I went to the supermarket and bought a huge striped watermelon. About a thirty-pounder. The children were all in bed while

I stealthily took the watermelon and sort of attached it to a vine in the garden.

The next day was Saturday, and I could hardly wait to trick them. When they were awake I got them all together and took them to the garden. When we got close enough for them to see the huge melon, they screamed with joy and shouted, "Is it ripe?"

"Well, let's see," I said in reassuring manner. Then I walked to the melon, bent over, and thumped it with my finger. I smiled at the kids as I said, "It sounds ripe to me."

"How did it get so big so fast?" they asked.

"Well, your dad just knows how to raise watermelons," I replied.

The next day my oldest son, who had done some analytical thinking, told them all that I had bought the melon at the store and secretly placed it in the garden. I knew that I had been found out. I broke down and laughed and laughed and shouted, "I tricked you little kids. I'm smarter than you, and I tricked you."

They tried to catch me and beat me up, but I ran away. Still laughing.

They all still remember the day that I tricked them. However, none of them are humble enough to acknowledge to their children that they were really tricked.

My grandchildren also love to hear about the way that I would trick their mom or dad on New Year's Eve. In the late afternoon I would cleverly set the clock ahead three hours. Then, when the clock would strike twelve midnight, we would get out the pans and the big spoons and bang the spoons on the pans to celebrate the arrival of the new year. But it wouldn't actually be midnight. It would really be nine o'clock. That way I could trick them into going to bed early on New Year's Eve. Incidentally, my children now tell my grandchildren that they weren't tricked at all. But they were.

I also tell my grandchildren of how I used to tell their mom or dad that hamburgers were better than steak. So when we would go out to dinner, while I ordered steak they would order hamburgers. Finally my oldest son decided that steak was better than hamburgers. And they all learned that I had been tricking them.

My grandchildren love these stories of how Grandpa was smarter than their dad or mom.

Now I notice my children trying to trick their little children, just as I tricked them when they were little. But of course they are not as clever as I was, and my grandchildren are too smart to be tricked.

So, being a trickster at heart, I now trick my grandchildren. I trick some of my grandchildren into believing that I am one of the world's richest men.

How do I do this? I do it by taking them to McDonald's every time I go to their house. They are amazed that anyone has enough money to go to McDonald's anytime they want. I also take them to the dollar store and tell them to get anything they want that costs a dollar or less. To them this represents great and unlimited wealth.

Recently I overheard my little grandson telling his friend, "My grandpa is one of the richest men in the world."

I love them to think that, because I always wanted to be rich. Or at least to have somebody think that I was rich. But just as my children learned that I didn't grow the watermelon, my grandchildren are getting to the age when they know that even though I'm richer than some of their parents, there are people in the world who have more money than I do. Oh, well! Such a wealthy reputation was good while it lasted.

In a way, I'm glad that I'm not rich. Being rich would be hard if you also had grandchildren. Because then you would want to give them and their parents too much. You would never want them to go without anything. If they wanted a bigger house, you would be tempted to help them get it. If they wanted four-wheelers, you would buy them four-wheelers. Now, there isn't much wrong with that except that it really isn't what grandparents are for. McDonald's? Yes. The dollar store? Yes. But big things that parents have a right and a responsibility to provide? No. Of course we help—when even a little house is beyond their means and a little help from the grandparents can make up the difference after all they can do.

You who are rich can wrestle with the problems of wealth. It isn't a problem for me, because, as my grand-children will learn soon enough, Grandpa really isn't the richest man in the world—or the town or even the neigh-borhood.

But there is something that you can't trick anybody about, because even little children can see through these tricks if you try to trick them. That is the quality of being a good person. You can't trick them into thinking that you are good if you are not.

They must never find out that you ever even attempted to trick them into thinking that you were good. You must never pretend to be good, even when they are little. You always just plain need to *be* good.

Being good is far more important than being rich. And as the grandchildren get older, they need to find out more and more that Grandpa is good. Being good, and especially being good to children, is what grandfathers are for. The greatest gift a grandpa can give to a grandchild is to be a role model of goodness. There is no way that you can give too much goodness to them.

The greatest honor that ever came to me happened when my little grandson Ryan was just learning to talk. He had learned some words such as *ball* and *book* and *light*. He also, of course, knew *daddy* and *momma*. And he had quickly learned the word *grandpa* after I had said it to him fifty-four times. But to that point in time, he had not mastered the art of putting two words together.

The next time I came to see him, he and I were playing on the floor. We had been laughing together and sort of wrestling around. We paused for a moment and looked at each other. Something went between us—something that can happen only in a family. He then spoke very slowly and with great deliberation. He said, "G-ra-n-dpa . . . g-o-o-d."

His words melted my heart. His mother, who also heard the words, was reduced to tears. I took him in my arms and thanked him. It was, as I said, a great moment for me.

My intense desire is that when I finally leave this earth his words will not change and he will not have changed his mind but will feel and say, "Grandpa good."

We grandpas have our problems, don't we? When we were twenty, we thought that older people are not tempted to be dishonest or to lose their integrity or to be unkind. But age doesn't make our quest to be good any easier.

But grandchildren sure do give us motivation to be good. Maybe in our younger years we let our children down at times because of our immaturity. But we are older now, and wiser. And we know now, more than ever, that these little ones who are dearer to us than life itself need us to be good. We know that we must never let them down. We must never do anything that would cause them to ever lose their feeling that Grandpa is good. It won't matter if they can't say that Grandpa is rich. But it will have deep consequences to them if they can't say, "Grandpa is good."

If the whole world seemed to turn against them, the one thing that they ought to be able to count on is Grandpa. Sometimes Mother and Father can't work things out, and they go their separate ways. Then, more than ever, Grandfather needs to be a rock of loyalty and love to the grandchildren.

Jesus said it well when he said: "But whoso shall offend one of these little ones which believe in me, it were better for him that a millstone were hanged about his neck, and that he were drowned in the depth of the sea" (Matthew 18:6).

As grandpas we must never be guilty of any abuse to anyone who believes in us as do these little grandchildren.

Some of us grandpas aren't too talented. We aren't the most charming people in the world. We don't know how to tell fascinating stories. We aren't too good at expressing love with tender words. That is all right. The kind of goodness we are talking about now is not that kind of goodness. It is just quiet goodness. Goodness that is felt rather than said. Goodness that is not just there now and then but is constant and which is marrow-of-the-bone deep.

We can fake a watermelon, and we can fake midnight, and we can fake riches, but we can't fake goodness. Goodness just won't allow itself to be felt where it is not present.

Be good, Grandpa. Your goodness and your love can bring peace and direction to a grandchild in a most difficult world.

Chapter Seven

Grandpa's Time

I used to love basketball with a deep passion. I mean, I really liked it. It took precedence over ninety percent of the rest of my life's activities.

That is the way I felt when my second little grandchild, Katie, was two years old. Katie is a little redhead, but other than that she is a typical little child.

I was tending her on a Saturday afternoon while her parents were at the movies. I stayed home gladly with her because she was due for a nap and there was an NCAA tournament game on. Ralph Samson was the big star at the time. I loved to see him play, and this was a semifinal game. I was keyed up about watching it from the beginning to the end.

But, to my great distress, Katie would not go to sleep.

She cried and begged to get up from her crib. I could deal with that because I could hold her on my lap while I watched the game. That worked until just before tip-off. But then I was greatly distressed because she went to the door and began an impassioned appeal to go outside. I tried everything that I could think of to dissuade her from wanting to go to a place where I could not see the TV. But it was no use; I had to go with her.

It was then that a miracle occurred. A genuine miracle. For as we walked down the front steps to the sidewalk, I realized that the game would still be played even if I wasn't there to watch it. That profound thought led to another one. And that was the amazing realization that I really didn't care as much as I had thought I would about not being able to see the game. Holding Katie's tiny hand and having her look up at me caused me to sense that what I was doing was much more important than seeing a ball swish through a net.

As we walked along it was a clear, wonderful, early spring day. At every house we passed, Katie would turn in and walk up the sidewalk to the porch. Arriving at the doorstep, she would turn back. I never gave her any direction, I just went wherever she wanted to go. Finally, after going a block away, she turned back toward home. Again we went up each sidewalk. Then we came to a little ditch. And I, to her great amusement, threw some rocks into the water. She laughed at each splash, and so did I. Finally we arrived back home. The game had just ended. To my surprise, I realized that the same team had won who would have won had I been there to watch. To this day I don't know who the winner was. But I can see in my mind every house that Katie led me to, and I can still see the rocks splashing into the water. I can still feel her tiny hand holding on to my extended finger. And when I see those things in my mind, it is like being in heaven.

Give the grandkids your time. Put aside some of your golf, some of your car repairs and the things that you do in your shop. Turn the TV off and experience the miracle of the way that you feel when you go for a walk with your little Katie or Gary or Kevin or Emma.

The publisher wanted me to hurry this book along so they would be able to get it printed by the deadline. But, I'd get writing stuff like I just wrote. It would put me in a special mood. I'd put the papers aside, and I would go see the grandkids.

I'm an artist. I love to paint watercolor paintings. When my children were little, I used to long for the day when they would be grown and I'd have time to paint without ignoring them. Finally that time has come. My youngest son, Markie, is now twenty-five years old. But, sadly or happily, my painting is still largely waiting, because now I have grandchildren.

I just know that inside me is a great painting. A painting that would make me famous. I used to dream that someday I'd paint that painting which would hang near the Mona Lisa. But so far my paintings aren't even good enough to make the Mona city art show. Now, the problem isn't a matter of talent. I have that. At least that is what I tell myself. It is a matter of time. Because when I have time to paint, it is also a great time to go see the children and the grandchildren.

But I have helped produce a picture that people rave

about. It is indeed a masterpiece. It hangs on my front room wall. It is a photo of Marilyn and me, our children, and our grandchildren. It is the greatest picture that I will have ever helped to create.

I have a passion for painting. Your passion could be for reading, for gardening; it might even be a passion for a green and perfectly groomed lawn. Lay those passions aside and go see the grandkids. That is the passion that will be eternally significant.

Now, don't get the idea that I don't know that we should live our own lives and let the kids and the grandkids live theirs. We shouldn't give up all our interests for someone else's. We deserve to have time to ourselves. I know all of that. But you and I both know that anything else, I mean everything else, is not even in the same ballpark with the importance of family.

Recently I wrote a letter to each of our children telling them when Marilyn and I would come to their home for family home evening during the next several months. I wrote, "We want to come, but we do not want to be pests." My son Devin saw the letter before I sent it out. He asked, "What is this nonsense?" He then scratched out the words about being pests. He chastised me, but I didn't get upset. Instead I felt glad in my heart. We grandpas don't want to be pests. And we won't be by visiting often. We only become pests if when we visit we stay too long. When you visit your children and their families, go home before they want you to. By doing that, they will always want you to come back. One day there may come a time when you will have to stay longer than either they or you desire. But even then, you will not be a pest.

I used to wonder, when I was younger, if I'd love my grandchildren as much as I love my children. Of course the answer is no. It is the first-line responsibility we have for our children that makes us love them so intensely. We don't have that day-and-night responsibility with our grandchildren. Thus, the love is different. It is not as intense, but it is just as deep. And the more we go to see them and go for a walk with them or see them in a dance festival or see them play ball or read them a book or go to a Disney film with them, the sweeter our love becomes. And you know, as I think of it, I nearly love those little grandchildren as much as I love my children. One thing— they seem a little bit cuter than my own children did.

Chapter Eight

Grandpa's New Sons and Daughters

On one occasion Marilyn was in Salt Lake City. That left my son Mark and me to fend for ourselves. When dinnertime came we made a feeble attempt to find something in the fridge to eat. Soon discouraged by the effort required to fix a meal, we got in the car and headed to an elegant fast-food place.

When we finally settled at our table and began to eat, Mark said, "I have some news for you, Father."

"What is it?" I asked eagerly.

"You have to guess," he responded.

"Is it some athletic thing?" I asked.

"No, it is not an athletic thing."

"Is it something that happened to you?"

"Yes, it involved me," he replied.

"Does it have to do with school?"

"No, nothing to do with school."

"Is it some accomplishment of yours?"

He smiled and said, "Yes, it will be quite an accomplishment."

"Does it have to do with romance?" I coyly asked.

"Yes, it does," he said with a look of love in his eyes.

"Does it have to do with Marilee?"

"Yes, it does."

"Are you engaged?" I asked, hoping against hope.

"Not yet, but within a week we will be."

I was so filled with joy that I could scarcely eat my fish and chips.

Mark is our last child. When he marries they all will be married.

We love Marilee.

I felt a bit like Abraham when he looked forward to the upcoming marriage of his son Isaac.

We told that story in chapter four. You recall the beautiful story of how Rebekah was found for Isaac in a distant land—how Abraham sent his trusted servant to the land of his relatives to find a bride for Isaac. You recall how Rebekah came to the well where the servant waited. He asked for a drink, which she graciously gave him. Then she gave his camels a drink also.

That is the kind of damsel Marilee is.

As a matter of fact, with the addition of Marilee we will have a total of five such daughter-in-law damsels in our family: Jackie, Julie, Marci, Jodi, and Marilee.

The Bible tells us that when the servant returned with Rebekah:

Isaac went out to meditate in the field at the eventide: and he lifted up his eyes, and saw, and, behold, the camels were coming.

And Rebekah lifted up her eyes, and when she saw Isaac, she lighted off the camel.

For she had said unto the servant, What man is this that walketh in the field to meet us? And the servant had said, It is my master: therefore she took a vail, and covered herself. . . .

And Isaac brought her into his mother Sarah's tent, and took Rebekah, and she became his wife; and he loved her. (Genesis 24:63–67.)

The Bible doesn't mention it, but the imagination of my heart tells me that Abraham was filled with pure joy at all this.

I can see him watching the camels come and holding back and letting Isaac go out alone to the caravan. I'm sure he shielded his eyes from the sun so as to get a good look at this person who was to now become a member of his family.

I can see him a few minutes later as he graciously greeted Rebekah. I'm sure that he was filled with deep emotion as he sensed that his son was truly blessed to have such a choice bride.

I suppose Abraham performed the eternal marriage for this radiant couple. Or maybe he had his trusted friend Melchizedek do so. At any rate, I'm sure that it was Abraham's best day so far when he had the comfort of knowing that this faithful, generous woman would be the wife of his dear son and the mother of his grandchildren.

I have many joys in life. Some of the supreme joys are my daughters-in-law. I sense—and I think I am right when I say this—that they adore me. And I know without any doubt that they are as dear to me as are their husbands. They treat me as though I were a king. Going into each of their homes is, for me, like entering heaven.

Then there are Paul and Steve and Kelly, the husbands of my daughters.

Paul can fix things. He can fix cars, lamps, lawnmowers, leaky water taps, and everything else that has a moving part. In a family of people who are quite helpless in the presence of a broken machine, Paul is worth his weight in handyman dollars.

But as bad as our family needed a fix-it man, we needed Steve even worse. For you see, Steve is a psychologist. He is still trying to figure us all out and see if he can get us over our odd behaviors.

Then there is Kelly. What is he good for? I guess he is just good for being good. He makes us all want to be like him, and he also knows all the football and baseball scores for this year and back as far as 1905.

I write of these wonderful people who came to our home through marriage, because they are such a grand dimension to my experience as the grandpa to their children.

One of the things I didn't know about family life was just how dear these people would be to me. I just didn't know how happy it would make me to have them in our family.

I don't criticize my children or my other children to

whom they are married. I just applaud them and cheer for them and affirm them. I try with all my heart not to meddle in their affairs, especially in the way that they raise my little grandchildren. Marilyn and I had our shot at being in charge of our own little children, and now we give our children the right to raise theirs. That is not difficult, because I am amazed at how well each couple does. Even little Conyor Bob and Chester, our wildest and most flighty grandchildren, are treated the way I would want them treated.

One time I got a little out of line in this area of meddling in the discipline of our grandchildren, and my daughter-in-law got after me pretty good.

This is what happened. My son and I were in the front room after a lovely Mother's Day dinner. My two little granddaughters Eliza and Annie were dancing about the front room, where my son and I were talking. We should have told them not to be so rambunctious, but we didn't. Finally one of them bumped into a table and knocked a family picture off the table. Her mother heard the picture hit the floor and came in. She quickly began to scold the little girls.

I had seen a movie once where the teacher took the blame when a little child got into trouble with the principal. I liked what that teacher had done, and so I jokingly said to the mother, "I was the one who was dancing, and I accidentally bumped the table."

This firm mother turned to me and quickly said, "You hush up, Grandpa." I knew that I was in trouble, and I hushed right up. It caused me to resolve again to stay out of those kinds of matters and stay in my role as the storyteller, the swing pusher, the bird pointer outer, and the ice cream buyer.

I know that in many families marriages don't work out. This is a great tragedy for the couple and for the children. And to a lesser (but maybe sometimes a greater) degree, it is a tragedy for the grandparents.

Sometimes the little grandchildren come to live with Grandpa and Grandma. Sometimes the grandparents become the parents. And they do a wonderful job of it.

In other cases the divorce results in bitter feelings between the couple. And it is natural that the grandparents take the side of their son or daughter. I know that I'm on deeply sensitive ground, but I hope Grandpa will not get bitter at either parent. I hope Grandpa will understand. I hope Grandpa will know that the best thing he can do for his grandchildren is to keep loving both of the grandchildren's parents. That could be the only binding power the children will feel for their tie to the former union of their two parents.

So, Grandpa, if one of your in-law sons or daughters does or says something that could offend you, step aside and let the negative energy pass by. Let the matter die before it is even born. Keep loving your grandchildren's parents. Never speak ill of them. If we look for it, there is something good about each of us. Look only for the good qualities in those who are now or who were once in your family portrait.

To my eight new sons and daughters, I proclaim, "Thank you for making it possible for me to know the great joy of being Grandpa."

Chapter Nine

When Grandpa Was
a Little Kid

Recently my grandson Tyler looked at me quizzically as we rode along a country road and said, "Grandpa, how does it feel to be old?"

Because we grandpas will forever think of ourselves as young, we fail to realize that in the minds of our grandchildren we are really quite ancient.

But although we would never agree that we are old, we have to admit that we have been around for a long time. And in our days we have seen and done some interesting things. Our grandchildren love to hear about those things. They especially like stories which begin with the words, "When Grandpa was a little kid . . ."

Once I was riding along in a car with four little

grandchildren and their parents. The children were a bit restless, and so I decided to see what I could do to entertain them. I told them the following story, which really seemed to touch their hearts:

> When Grandpa was a little kid, school lunch only cost three cents a day. But usually all that you got was a little bottle of milk and a bowl of soup.
>
> One day, I went through the line and got my soup and milk and started to walk to a table to eat. But as I walked along, the tray tipped and the bowl of soup slid along the tray and then fell to the cement floor. The bowl shattered and the soup made a big, messy puddle. Every student looked over at me. I was so embarrassed I could hardly stand it. My brother, who was two years older than me, laughed and laughed. I thought that I would die of shame right there in the lunchroom.
>
> One of the ladies who was in charge gave me some rags and a broom and told me to clean it up. It took me several minutes to do so, and those moments were the longest ones in my life.
>
> After that I was always really careful when I carried my soup to my table.

When I finished the story, the four little grandchildren were very quiet. Somehow they had each identified with how bad I had felt on that day.

That started me on kind of a roll, and I told them my famous Valentine's Day story.

> When Grandpa was a little kid, they made really pretty valentines. These valentines were not the kind that come

on a big card from which you kind of punch out several little cards. Some had pretty lace around the edges, and some had moving parts. If you moved an arm the eye would wink. The teacher would make a big heart-shaped box with a slot in the top where you could put the valentines which you wanted to send to members of the class. The box was always beautiful.

All this made Valentine's Day one of my favorite days to look forward to. But the day itself was not my best day. Because, you see, back then you did not have to give a valentine to every person in the class. You could just give them to the ones you really liked.

So on Valentine's Day the big heart box would be opened, and the valentines would be passed out. Some students would get one from every other member of the class. But I would only get three or four. And none of them would have lace or moving parts. I'd feel so bad that I would want to cry.

The grandchildren were almost in tears at this story.

They seem to like the stories about things that made Grandpa sad more than any other stories.

But I also tell them happy stories, like the one about the duck.

When Grandpa was a little kid, there was a late spring snowstorm. I was sitting looking out the window watching it snow, when I was surprised to see a little baby yellow duck running down the dirt road in front of our house. In an instant, I ran to the duck, scooped it up into my hands, and headed for the warm house.

I held the duck in my lap. Because I had found the duck

when it was so young, it decided that I was its mother. I kept that duck for three years. It would follow me around like a little dog follows its master. I loved that duck with all my heart.

The children liked that story. They love stories from the olden days that are told by Grandpa.

So tell your olden-day stories to your grandchildren. You may not be a great storyteller. That doesn't matter. They will listen if you are riding in a car or if there isn't something else that they want to do.

For Christmas one year I got a tape recorder and recorded every olden-day story that I could remember. I told story after story of little things that had happened to me. One story led to the memory of another. I gave each grandchild a tape of those stories, and they often listen to them when they go to bed. My stories put them right off to sleep.

I give talks to groups of people. Sometimes these talks are recorded. My granddaughter Emily has every talk tape I have made. She listens to them every night. She can tell the stories that I have told, and she can do it word for word. I love to have her tell my stories back to me.

Now her brother, Ryan, and her sisters, Laura and Heather, listen to these tapes. The other night Julie, their mother, called and said, "Grandpa, I just wanted you to know that you are in stereo in our house tonight. Your voice is coming from all our children's bedrooms. Each child has a different talk tape of Grandpa's stories playing in their room."

Telling your personal olden-day stories is a good way

to leave a bit of your history to your grandchildren. You should do that, you know. We are all encouraged to write our personal histories. I'm trying to get a law passed making it a felony for any grandpa to die before he has written his personal history or at least told thirty-seven stories on tape about when he was a little kid.

If you write or record on tape your olden-day stories, not only will you be able to teach your grandchildren but also they will be able to tell your stories to their children.

In my heart I see a vision of the time when my little grandson Tanner will be a father. He will be sitting around a table in his humble home with his beautiful wife and my great-grandchildren. He will be telling them stories because he will have a book with my stories in it. I can hear the children saying, "Daddy, tell us more stories about Great-Grandpa George."

Then this wonderful father, my grandson, will say, "Here is a picture of Grandpa George."

One of the children will say, "I thought you said that he was handsome."

"Well, he always said that he was. No one else thought that he was. He always joked like that."

Then my grandson will say, "Listen to this story about his Studebaker."

The children will ask, "What is a Studebaker, Daddy?"

"Well, it was a car that was made a long time ago. The front and the back looked exactly the same. Grandpa George never really owned a Studebaker. But he always dreamed of having one. A Studebaker was his dream car. He worked really hard to get enough money to buy a Studebaker, but he could never earn enough to do so. But while he worked, it was easy for him to sweat and labor, because in his mind he wasn't thinking of how hard the work was. Instead he was always dreaming of his Studebaker. This is what he said":

> I wanted that Studebaker so bad that it was always on my mind. I could see myself driving it. All the girls in town would want to ride in it with me, and I would be the most popular boy in the whole big town of American Fork. I could see myself, as plain as day, one day driving my Studebaker up the hill towards American Fork High School. I'd whiz past all the other young people who were walking to school. All of them would wish that I would stop and give them a ride. The two prettiest girls in town would see me going by, and one of them would say to the other, "There goes old George."
>
> The other one would reply, "How do you know he is going? He might be coming. You can't tell in a Studebaker."

The children will ask, "Did Grandpa George ever really have a Studebaker?"

"Oh, no, he didn't. But he didn't mind, because he said it was more fun to have a Studebaker in your mind than it was to have one in your garage."

One of the children will speak up and say, "I love Grandpa George. Tell us more stories about him."

"Here is another of his stories":

> I was in the army, but I was never in a battle. When we'd be marching I'd try very hard to not make any mistakes, because we had a real mean sergeant. If you made a mistake while you were marching and went right when

you were supposed to go left, he would call you bad names. I didn't want to be called bad names by the mean sergeant.

Each night when I'd pray, I'd say, "Heavenly Father, please help me to march good so that the mean sergeant won't get angry and call me those bad names that he calls the other soldiers."

Then one Saturday we were standing in formation in front of our barracks, waiting to be dismissed. I was very happy that we would have the afternoon off, and I was thinking about that instead of about marching. The mean sergeant shouted, "Left face!"

I got confused and did a right face, and that made it so everyone else was facing away from the mean sergeant but I was standing face-to-face with him.

My heart pounded with fear, for now I knew that the mean sergeant would call me bad names, just like he called all of the other soldiers bad names when they made mistakes.

But as I looked into the mean sergeant's eyes, he couldn't seem to even talk. Then in a really soft voice he said, "Private Durrant, turn around." Then he said, "Company dismissed!"

Everybody shouted with happiness and ran toward the barracks. But instead of running and shouting, I quietly and slowly walked away. I was very happy that Heavenly Father made it so that the mean sergeant could not call me bad names.

I learned that if you pray, Heavenly Father will protect you against things like the words of the mean sergeant. That is why I hope all of my grandchildren and their children will always say their prayers every night and every morning.

My grandchildren will say, "I want to be sure to pray like Grandpa George did when he prayed that the mean sergeant wouldn't call him bad names."

It would be nice to leave your children an inheritance of a million dollars so that they could all go to college and on missions and maybe even have a Studebaker. But it is much better to leave them a dream of doing these things. For a dream is all that is needed. It is better to have a dreamer's license in your wallet than to have a wallet bulging with money. If you have a dream, everything else will take care of itself.

Leave your grandchildren stories about your life and your dreams and your faith and your love. You don't have to brag. Some of us don't have much to brag about. But if they know that you spilled your soup once and that you didn't get many valentines and that you didn't really have a Studebaker and that the mean sergeant couldn't say bad things about you because you prayed, then you have given your grandchildren your greatest gift: not anything you had but everything you are.

Chapter Ten

Grandpa: A Patriarch

As one settles into his grandfather years, the word *patriarch* takes on greater meaning.

My dictionary says of the word *patriarch:* "The father or head of a family like Abraham, Isaac and Jacob. Any very old or dignified man. A high dignitary who has the right to invoke and pronounce blessings."

So according to that, my fellow grandpas, we are patriarchs. We may not think we are old, but the grandchildren think we are. So it is through their eyes that we now look at our age.

You may not feel that you are dignified, but in our own way you and I really are quite dignified, if we overlook some of our undignified ways.

The last part of what my dictionary said is what really

impressed me: "A high dignitary who has the right to invoke and pronounce blessings."

I'm sure that you, like me, are not a high dignitary out in the city or even in the neighborhood. But in our own families we are quite high dignitaries. This was brought to my mind recently when I made a surprise visit to my son Devin's house.

I have a way of ringing the doorbell so that the children know it is me. I push the doorbell button not just once but again and again and again. It just keeps ringing until they get to the door. But even before they get to the door they know that it is me. From inside the house I can hear their excited voices shouting, "It's Grandpa! It's Grandpa!"

On this day when I came to their house, they just mobbed me on the porch. Two of the four were each clinging to my legs. One had her arm around my waist, and little Ryan was pleading with me to pick him up.

Now, to me that qualifies as the type of greeting a high dignitary would get. Then Julie, the mother, shouted, "Grandpa George, what a wonderful surprise!" So it isn't just with the kids that I'm a high dignitary—it is with the parents too.

Of course, it helps, if you want to be a really high dignitary, to have some candy in your pocket. But that isn't really necessary. All that is necessary is to be good and to be there and to tell a story or two and to love them.

But now I want to go to the last part of that which my dictionary said: "The right to invoke and pronounce blessings."

One day when I was standing in a small grove of trees

near the Provo River, I began to think of my children and my grandchildren. I decided that I would like to go to their homes and give each of them a blessing. It wouldn't be a Patriarchal Blessing, because I am not a Patriarch. It would instead be a patriarchal blessing, because I am a patriarch.

So, I wrote each family a letter telling them that I would like to come to their home on a special night and give them each a blessing.

The first to respond were Devin and Julie. On the appointed night, when Marilyn and I arrived, we were greeted in the high dignitary fashion to which we have become accustomed. Devin seemed more sober than usual. He shook hands with me and called me Father. When he called me Father, I sensed that he knew the full significance of what was about to happen. Dads and grandpas can do certain things, but other things are reserved for fathers and grandfathers. It is by being a good dad and grandpa that we earn the right to, at times, be called Father or Grandfather.

After visiting for a while the sacred time for the blessings had come.

I decided to start with the youngest child and go to the oldest. Ryan was first, and although he was only three years old he seemed to sense what was happening. Then Heather, then Laura, then Emily (my little disciple), then mother Julie, who longed to have another baby but who had not been able to conceive (we made a special mention of that in her blessing), and then father Devin. As Devin stood up following his blessing, he was crying. He was deeply touched. Then Devin gave his mother a blessing, and then he gave me one. The things that he said in my blessing gave me much hope for the future.

We ate a piece of cake, but the mood in the home was more like the temple than it had ever been before.

My oldest son, Matthew, and his family live in Salt Lake City, and we don't get there as often as I would like. It was the Christmas holiday week. Marilyn had gone to their home the week before to tend the six children for a few days while Matt and Jackie had gone out of town. So on New Year's Day, Sunday, when I suggested that we go to see Matt and his family, she declined because she had just been there. I asked her if she would mind if I went without her. She assured me that she wouldn't mind at all.

So away I went. When I arrived, it was late Sunday afternoon. I rang the doorbell the way that high dignitaries do. The children and the little white dog ran to the door, shouting and barking. I was greeted with uncontrolled glee. It was difficult to tell who was happiest—me or the children. Or maybe it was Jackie, the mother. She always makes me feel as though, next to her husband and her father, I am the greatest man upon the face of the earth.

She took my coat and invited me to sit down. "What can I get you to eat?" she asked.

I assured her that anything would be fine. But she said, "No, you tell me what you want, and whatever it is, I'll make it for you."

She had made some soup, and it was just right. As I sat there eating with that family it was again just like being in heaven. I looked at Jacob, the fourteen-year-old computer whiz. (You have a grandchild who is a computer whiz—every grandfather does.) His quiet smile melted my heart. He has such respect for every good thing and for all people, including me, his grandpa. As I said earlier, he is to me as the biblical Jacob was to my hero Abraham. I looked at twelve-year-old Andrea, the tennis player, who seemed, as usual, to be so royal. I turned my gaze to Jessica, the one whose talent is so big that it hardly fits into her young body. I smiled at Ellie, who could get a patent on her pure version of love. I looked at three-year-old Mattie, the one who knows only joy, and last of all I looked at pretty little Kelsey.

When I had first arrived that day and come into the house, one-year-old Kelsey had not wanted to come to me. But I resolved that before I departed she would not go to anyone else but me.

After dinner Matt put *The Music Man* on the video machine because he knows that it is my favorite movie. It was bitter cold outside, but inside we were warm through and through. I held a child on each side of me. Kelsey kept watching me and wondering why everyone seemed to like me so much. Finally she decided to let me hold her. Holding a grandchild is so deeply moving. It seems like holding the past and the future and all that is dear. At times we would all get to our feet and dance with those who were dancing in the movie.

When the movie was over Matthew said, "Father, would you be willing to give us our blessings tonight before you go home?"

I agreed but I said, "I'm not going home tonight. I am going to sleep here." A cheer went up from all the children. A high dignitary would spend the night in their humble home. Jackie smiled and said, "We have a real good bed for you, Grandpa. You could stay for a week if you want. We'd all love that."

We left the family room and went into their beautifully decorated front room. Kelsey wanted me to carry her, and then she wanted to sit on my lap. Somehow she knew that I was not really a stranger. I was Grandpa. It seemed like she didn't discover that anew but remembered it from her past.

Before we began the blessings, I told the children about the government that we would have in heaven when we all got there. I said, "There won't be any mayors or governors or presidents in heaven. The government there will be a family government. In heaven we will have a patriarchal government. You will look to your father there as your respected patriarch. You will also look to your grandfather as a patriarchal leader. Each of you will govern yourself there, but we will be a family in heaven just at we are here, and that will be our government. So now as I give you a blessing it will be a blessing from one of your patriarchs, your grandfather."

Kelsey was first to receive her blessing. She wasn't overly impressed, because her father was holding her and my hands were on her head and she wondered what was going on. So her blessing was short.

Next came Mattie. His real name is Matthew George Durrant. I wanted him to be named George, after me, but the best I could get was for that to be his middle name. As I blessed him, I softly said his first name, "Matthew." Then

I said in a loud voice, "George." Then I added in a normal voice, "Durrant." He too was a bit restless and received a short but very meaningful blessing.

When I in turn blessed Ellie, Jessica, and Andrea, the blessings grew longer. A spirit of peace and love came into each of our hearts.

Finally it was time for Jacob's blessing. My oldest grandchild. I began his blessing the same way that I had begun all the others. I called him by name and then said, "As your grandfather I seal upon you all the blessings that your father has given to you as you have progressed through your life. And now, I add a special blessing to those blessings. As your grandfather, I will now listen to our Heavenly Father and tell you all the thoughts that come into my heart about your life and your eternal destiny."

Thought after thought poured into my heart, and I related them to this dear young man. I could feel the great love that our Heavenly Father has for him. As I felt these things I could scarcely speak. It was as if we were all in the very halls of heaven.

Then it was my privilege to give my dear daughter Jackie a blessing. It was very much a blessing of love and appreciation for her deep devotion to my son and to my grandchildren. In the blessing, more than at any other time, I was able to tell her how much I love her.

And finally my beloved son Matthew Burnham Durrant sat in the chair and received, as he had so often, a blessing at the hands of his father.

All the children wanted to have Grandpa receive a blessing, and so my son Matt gave me a blessing. After the blessings were over we sat and talked. Little Kelsey sat on my lap and I was happy.

I'll visit this family again. But never again will my visit be like the night that I gave them each a grandfather's blessing—blessings that will be answered to the very letter.

Near the bed that they so generously provided, I knelt down and thanked Heavenly Father for the joy of being a patriarch, a high dignitary, a grandpa, with the power to invoke and pronounce blessings.

The next morning we had hotcakes because Jackie knows that I love hotcakes. Little Kelsey sat on my lap while I ate. Her mother said to her, "Get down for a minute, Kelsey, while Grandpa eats." But she would not budge. Her dad said, "I'll get her." He tried but she clung to me and couldn't be moved. She opened her mouth, and I gently placed a piece of pancake inside, and we were both happy.

Chapter Eleven

Grandpa's Dream

While I served as president of the Missionary Training Center in Provo, it was my sad responsibility to tell several missionaries of the death of a father or mother. As you would do, I made a fervent appeal to the Lord for his help, for myself and for the grieving young missionary.

Much more often than informing them of the passing of a parent, I told missionaries of the death of a grandparent. I felt that this would be easier. But in that, I was quite wrong.

I recall the first time that I informed a missionary of this sad news. I sat with a young elder in my office to inform him that his grandfather had died. I, of course, had a great concern and was as gentle and considerate as I could be.

I said, "My dear friend, it is my sad duty to tell you that your grandfather passed away last night."

His reaction, to a slight degree, surprised me. It shouldn't have, and it did not thereafter. But it did this first time. He started to cry. A seemingly endless flow of tears fell from his eyes. I sat in silence, sensing his deep emotional distress. When his gentle sobbing had almost stopped, I softly said, "Tell me about your grandfather."

Wiping the tears away, his eyes brightened as his mind filled with the memories of his living grandfather. A smile came upon his face as he began to speak. He told me of the experiences he had shared with his grandfather. They had spent time fishing and farming and just being together. He told me of how his grandfather had so often affirmed him when he felt discouraged and unimportant. He told me of the faith of his grandfather and of the love that his grandfather and grandmother had for each other. He told me many more sacred things about the relationship that he had with his grandpa.

I asked, "Was the news of the passing of your grandfather a surprise to you? Did you know that he was sick?"

"It was not a surprise," he replied. "Grandpa had been sick for more than a year. I knew that he wouldn't be there when I returned from my mission. Mom and Dad have cared for him in our home for the past two years. He couldn't talk the last several months, but he could listen, and I used to talk to him each day when I'd come home from school or work. He got so he could remember hardly anybody, but I could tell that somehow he could remember me."

With that he began to gently sob again. But then it appeared that a quiet revelation entered his heart, and the tears of this noble elder ceased. A perceptible glow of hope lighted his countenance. He sat up straighter in his chair and said, "At least now Grandpa and Grandma will be together again."

I asked with deep respect, "Do you really believe that?"

"I know that," he said. "Grandma and Grandpa taught me that."

After this young missionary left my office, I knelt among the sweet, sacred memories of what I had just heard and felt. I prayed that the Lord would continue to comfort this young grandson of a most noble grandfather. I prayed that I would leave such a legacy as this grandpa had done and that someday my grandson or granddaughter would speak of me as this missionary had spoken of him.

I guess I shouldn't say it, but I will anyway. I sure do hope that when I die I will have so lived that my family, especially my grandchildren, will cry the sweet tears of missing the fun, the encouragement, the faith, and the love of Grandpa.

My greatest dream is that through my stories and my deeds and most of all my love, their memories of me will allow the best parts of me to forever live on in their hearts. I hope that the mention or memory of my name will bring pleasant feelings to them forever. But more than desiring that my name live on, I hope that the qualities of integrity, honor, respect, love, and faith that I have tried to stand for and in which I have so dearly believed will abound in their souls forever.

My favorite family story, and the model after which I have fashioned my dream of the future of my family, came to me from a man I met in a distant state. At the time I had this experience I was a young father. I was on a speaking tour, and I stayed in this man's home. That night when all the others in the family had gone to bed, this father and I were conversing in a very heart-to-heart manner. On that unforgettable evening, he told me this story:

Two months ago we had a most amazing thing happen in our family. For years our family had wanted to go to Disneyland. This was the year we were to go. We had saved for this trip for several months. Now we had the money and the vacation time to go. Three weeks before we were to depart, we were sitting at the dinner table. There was a feeling of real gloom in our home. I tried to cheer everybody up, but I could not. We ate in that silence that sometimes falls upon families.

Finally my oldest son, seventeen years old, asked, "Why do we have to go to Disneyland?"

I about fell off my chair. Almost in anger, I said, "Now, just what do you mean by that? Have you and your friends planned something? You are getting so that nothing in the family is as important as being with your friends."

"No, it's not that," he said softly.

Again silence returned. Then my daughter said, "I know what Jed means, and I don't want to go to Disneyland either."

I was shocked. We had planned this trip for years.

I almost shouted as I said in a commanding voice, "Well, whether you want to or not, we are all going to Disneyland."

My wife put her hand gently on my hand and said, "Your brother phoned today and told us his children really felt bad that we were going to miss Kenley Creek this year to go to Disneyland. And I think that is what is troubling the children."

Then, almost in chorus, the children said, "We want to see our cousins. That is why we don't want to go to Disneyland."

I said, "Hey, look, I want to see the family too. But I only get so much vacation time, and we all decided it would be Disneyland. The family goes to Kenley Creek every year. We went there last year, and we'll go there next year, but this year we decided on Disneyland. Of course, if you all want to change the plans, well . . . I'd sooner see my brothers and sisters. But I thought this time we would do what you wanted to do."

My oldest son, who is known for his tough-guy attitude, seemed near tears as he asked, "Can we change, Dad?"

So we changed plans. I phoned my brother, and while we were talking I told him that we had decided to go to Kenley Creek. I could hear him shouting to his children, "Your cousins are coming to Kenley Creek!"

Our children were happy again.

Then this father told me the story of Kenley Creek.

When my father and mother were young we did not have much money. We couldn't go on vacation to any place that cost a lot. So every year Mom and Dad would pack the wooden grub box with all kinds of food. We'd tie the old canvas tent to the top of the 1947 Ford. All us children would pile in like sardines in a can, and off we would go to the mountains and to Kenley Creek.

We did that every year. Finally my older brother got married. His wife was sort of a fancy, rich girl. She had been all over the country on vacations. We didn't think that she would go with us to Kenley Creek, but she did and she had the time of her life.

One by one we all got married, and every summer at a certain time we would all come home and drive up to Kenley Creek.

The year after Dad died, we wondered if we should go. But Mom said that Dad would want us to go and that he'd be there with us. And so we all went.

As the years passed, each of us brothers and sisters had children of our own. My brother could play the accordion, and each night under the moonlight of the Kenley Creek sky he played polkas and all the kids would dance with their cousins.

Finally Mom died. But every year at Kenley Creek, in the quiet of the mountain evening, it seemed like Mom and Dad would come back and sit by the campfire with all of us. With the eyes of our hearts we could see them smile as they watched the grandkids dance and eat the watermelon that had been cooled by the cold waters of the stream. We brothers and sisters would talk of the times gone by, and Mom and Dad would just listen.

We all were a family, and we loved each other more and more as the years passed by.

When we decided to go to Disneyland, I guess I just didn't know how much these family ties meant to the children. We knew how much it meant to us but not to them.

So we changed our minds and went to Kenley Creek. We did so because being with our family meant more than all the Disneylands in the world.

So the Kenley Creek model became symbolic to me of that which I wanted most in my life. I just wanted a family wherein all the family members liked each other. A family where each member wanted to come home. A family that liked to be together.

As time goes by, it is easy for family members to have a falling out over some little thing or other. Sometimes little things become bigger and bigger, and pretty soon a family kind of falls apart.

Sometimes when Grandma and Grandpa move on to the eternal world, the rest of the family doesn't get together as often as they used to. And maybe that is all right. But to me it isn't all right. Brothers and sisters still need each other, no matter how old or how independent they become. And cousins need cousins. And children need uncles and aunts, and uncles and aunts need nieces and nephews. There is something about the connection to relatives that lies, sometimes dormant, in human hearts, and if nourished these inherited feelings will bloom into the purest and most enduring kind of love—the kind of love that comes from a shared heritage.

As life goes by, we will always find time for friends, and that is as it should be. But often we forget our family, and that is as it shouldn't be.

This desire to strengthen family ties seems to intensify as we become more mature in years. Perhaps that is why Marilyn and I recently wrote this letter to our children and grandchildren:

> Dear Family,
>
> Please carefully consider the following dream that we as grandparents have tried to put on paper. Study it with your children; revise it so that you feel you can really support it. Send us your thoughts on how it can be improved. We feel that if we all share the same dream, it will surely come true.
>
> When we all have agreed, we will call it "Our Family Dream."

This, then, is that dream:

> We will love all other family members, and we will do the things that people who love each other do. Namely:
>
> — We will visit each other as often as possible.
> — We will try to attend the yearly family activities.
> — We will pray for each other.
> — We will rejoice in the success of other family members.
> — We will be emotionally and spiritually supportive of one another.
> — We will each have personal integrity and bring honor to the family.
> — We, when we speak of other family members, will do so as if they were present.
>
> To help our dream come true, we will do things together. Whenever possible all family members will attend the following five annual family activities:

Overnight Family Camp Out: The date will be in June. Uncle Warren will be in charge of the food and the fun. So you know that it will be fun.

Overnight Olympic Games, Genealogical Report, and Talent Show: This will be held at Matt's estate and will be under his direction. There will be games and gold medals for all. Tennis will, of course, be featured. The genealogy report will be in the evening and will be under the direction of George and Marilyn. The talent show will be glorious. We will sleep outside or in Jackie's schoolroom. This date will be in August.

Backyard of Fire: This will be held at the old family home. It will include dinner and fireworks and Warren's famous marching music. This date will be on the evening of the Fourth of July.

Christmas Party: This will be held at various places to be determined each year. The date will also be chosen each year.

Family Temple Session: This will be held on a Saturday morning between Marilyn's and George's birthdays. Usually the second Saturday in October. We will all go out to dinner after the session.

Note: If any of the children live away from Utah, they will come home when they can to be at these events, and Grandma and Grandpa will visit them twice each year.

I can envision myself at each of these activities. I can see Warren giving the grandchildren a ride between the sagebrush on his four-wheeler. I can see us all sitting around a campfire in the west desert, roasting marshmallows. I can see us at Matt's watching the grandchildren running and jumping and each one receiving a gold medal. I can see us watching the Chinese fireworks colorfully lighting up our backyard as the red and green glow is reflecting in the children's eyes. I can see all of us at the Christmas party, exchanging gifts and speaking of the birth so long ago in the stable. I can see us talking of family history, of our ancestors, of our heritage. I can see us all dressed in white in the temple. I can feel on my lap the newest little grandchildren who have just come to our family. I can feel the joy of holding them close and feeling the bond of family love.

Oh, yes, I see visions all the time. Not visions of angels but visions of family. And as long as I have those visions and those dreams, I can see into heaven itself.

Many years ago at a family home evening my daughter Marinda looked around the room and said joyfully, "Daddy, our whole family is here." That, in summary, is Grandpa's present and eternal dream. And I'm sure that you, my fellow grandpas, share that same dream for your family.

"Grandpa. Grandpa! *Grandpa!* Are you awake?" I hope you and I will forever be able to respond, "Yes! Yes! Yes!"